D1199336

Persian Cats

ABDO
Publishing Company
A Buddy Book
by
Julie Murray

VISIT US AT
www.abdopub.com

Published by Buddy Books, an imprint of ABDO Publishing Company, 4940 Viking Drive, Suite 622, Edina, Minnesota 55435. Copyright © 2005 by Abdo Consulting Group, Inc. International copyrights reserved in all countries. No part of this book may be reproduced in any form without written permission from the publisher.

Printed in the United States.

Edited by: Christy DeVillier
Contributing Editors: Matt Ray, Michael P. Goecke
Graphic Design: Maria Hosley
Image Research: Deborah Coldiron
Photographs: Corel, Eyewire Inc., Fotosearch, Ingram Publishing, PhotoSpin

Library of Congress Cataloging-in-Publication Data

Murray, Julie, 1969-
    Persian Cats/Julie Murray.
        p. cm. — (Animal kingdom. Set II)
    Includes bibliographical references and index.
    Contents: Cats — Persian cats — What they're like — What they look like — Senses — Care — Food — Kittens — Buying a kitten.
    ISBN 1-59197-330-9
        1. Persian cat—Juvenile literature. [1. Persian cat. 2. Cats.] I. Title.

SF449.P4M87 2003
636.8'32—dc21

                                        2002038543

Contents

Domestic Cats

There are many kinds of cats. Tigers are the biggest cats. Cheetahs are the fastest cats. One of the smallest cats is the rusty-spotted cat. All cats belong to a group called Felidae.

Domestic cats are related to wild cats. They became tame thousands of years ago. These tame cats still have their hunting skills. They can catch and kill mice, birds, and other animals.

Wild cats

Domestic Persian cat

Persian Cats

People around the world keep **domestic cats** as pets. There are more than 40 **breeds** of domestic cats. A few different breeds are Siamese, Russian blue, and Persian.

Persian is one of the oldest breeds. Some people believe Persian cats came from Persia. Today, Persia is a country called Iran.

Persian cats came to North America in the late 1800s. Many Americans kept Persians as pets in the early 1900s. Today, Persian cats are popular pets.

Many people have pet Persian cats.

What They Look Like

Persian cats are famous for their long, thick hair. They have short, flat noses and small ears. Persians have short legs and bushy tails.

Persian cats have long hair.

Persian cats can be different colors. Solid-colored Persians are only one color. They may be white, black, brown, silver-blue, cream, or lilac. Other Persians have two or more colors.

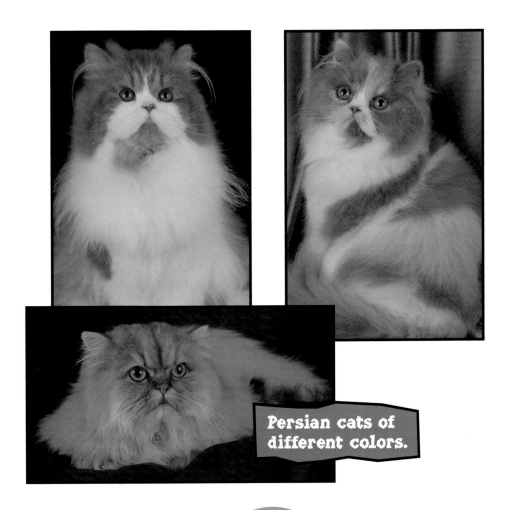

Persian cats of different colors.

Tabby Persian cats have stripes or patches of color. Himalayan Persians are a solid color with colored points. These points are a cat's face, ears, feet, and tail.

Himalayan Persian

Tabby Persian

Persians As Pets

Persian cats enjoy being around people. They get along well with children. They do not mind other animals. Persians are quiet, gentle, and loving.

Persian cats are not as active as other **breeds**. They may not often climb and jump to high places. Instead, Persians enjoy sitting on laps.

Persian cats make good pets.

13

Grooming And Care

Cats are clean animals. They **groom** themselves by licking their fur. Longhaired cats, such as Persians, need brushing, too.

Owners should brush their Persian cat every day. A wide-toothed comb helps to untangle their hair. Brushing with a soft brush is good, too. It removes dead hair that could lead to **hair balls**.

Like all cats, Persians will scratch things. Owners should trim their cat's claws. They can also train their cats to use scratching posts.

Persian cats can learn to use a scratching post.

Food

Cats need food and fresh water every day. Follow the feeding directions on the cat food. Be careful not to feed cats too much. Overweight cats can have health problems.

Cats need a **litter box** for their waste. Owners should clean the litter box every day.

Cats need food and water every day.

Do Cats Like Milk?

Many cats like to drink milk. But milk is not a good treat for cats.

Owners can buy cat treats from pet stores. A common cat treat is catnip. It is an herb. Many cats love to eat catnip. Some cats roll around in catnip, too.

Kittens

Baby cats are called kittens. As many as five Persian kittens may be born in a **litter**. Newborn kittens are blind. After a few weeks, they can see. Seven-week-old kittens can run and play.

Kittens need their mother's milk. They should not leave their mother before they are 12 weeks old. A healthy Persian cat can live for 15 years or more.

A Himalayan Persian kitten

Buying A Kitten

Some people adopt kittens from animal shelters. People go to pet stores for kittens, too.

A tabby Persian kitten

Before buying a kitten, look at it carefully. Does it have bright, clear eyes? Are its ears, nose, and fur clean? Is the kitten playful? If so, the kitten is probably healthy. To be sure, take the kitten to a **veterinarian**. This doctor helps pets stay healthy.

Important Words

breed a special group of cats. Cats of the same breed look alike.

domestic cats tame cats that make great pets.

groom to clean and care for.

hair ball hair that collects in a cat's belly.

litter the group of kittens born at one time.

litter box a place for house cats to leave their waste.

veterinarian a doctor for animals. A short name for veterinarian is "vet."

Web Sites

To learn more about Persian cats, visit ABDO Publishing Company on the World Wide Web. Web sites about Persian cats are featured on our Book Links page. These links are routinely monitored and updated to provide the most current information available.

www.abdopub.com

Index